Life's Prisoners

Life's

Prisoners

Darryl Lorenzo Wellington

Life's Prisoners
Copyright © 2017 Darryl Lorenzo Wellington
Winner, 2017 Turtle Island Poetry Award

Turtle Island Quarterly sponsors the annual Turtle Island Poetry Award. Awards are chosen by the editors. More information available at http://fourdirectionpoetry.wixsite.com/turtleisland

Cover image by Marya Kirby

First Flowstone Press Edition, October 2017
ISBN-13 978-1-945824-13-5

for
friends, family,
strangers, and others

Contents

Introduction, by Jared Smith	vii
Life's Prisoners	3
The World's First Black Gay Sci-fi Writer Devours the Classroom	4
The Crippled, Homeless Woman Speaks	5
The Third Trimester	6
The Daily Globe	7
Praise to the Window Blinds	8
Strippers Redux	9
New Letters. Old Advice.	11
Concerning the Recent Brutality	12
The Silence Before the Summer Storm	15
Parables for the End of the First Chapter.	16
Snow Blankets the Eastern Hills	17
Time Travel Haiku	18
Her Second Lives, and Such	20
Naming the Seasons	21
An Aubade	22
The Star Puppets	23
Come Join the Dark	25
DuBois at 90	26
To Ellison/Baldwin	27
The First Photographs	28
And They Say	29

Introduction

By Jared Smith

The racial hatred we see rising around us today...the black men and women and children being gunned down by white policemen, the rioting in our cities, the undocumented and the dreamers being locked up and shipped away, the statues to slavery that are honored by the KKK, the lights going out in our cities...all of this driven to a fever pitch today by a fat white con man in The White House rises from a long history of lies, delusions, fears, and failures. Regardless of what race we are or what our economic level or profession, we are all Life's Prisoners as long as we will tolerate this. We are allowing ourselves to be encaged by the sleepy rooms of our academies and institutions as well as by our own laziness and lack of intellectual curiosity, as Mr. Wellington points out in this important book. We have enabled what is happening to us now. It has been a long time coming, and we must address it. This book does so, powerfully and eloquently.

Life's Prisoners is a heroic book, a tightly crafted volume of poetry that grabs you by the collar, shouts in your face, disrespects what should be disrespected, and after waking you up, lets you know that all of us are prisoners in cages we have allowed to be constructed around us. The poems move from staccato fragments of the pictures of a young man's struggles, fear, and rage toward an indifferent world named and shaped by an unknowable elite, to impassioned pieces on what it is to be a man in such a world, to longer lined discussions of past and current history. We find pleas to Jesus, and references to Moses contrasted with cauldron-eyed phoenixes rising from their own ashes that foretell our future from our past. Through all its passion and anguish, it is a learned and welcoming book as well. It features warnings about life in a complex, duplicitous, and volatile society to a young black child; a tribute to the life and death of NYPD victim Eric Garner; a birthday poem celebrating the founder of the NAACP alongside an old friend who is a fellow Black Marxist historian; and a poem to Ralph Ellison and James Baldwin honoring their writing and their lives. And all the while, the poems dart and dance and cry like jazz—image and sound driven.

Let us not think that if we are not black, or if instead we are only impoverished or suffer from serious health issues, or psychological crises, this book does not concern us. It does, and although many of Mr. Wellington's historic references are to blacks and black history, he never identifies himself as other than a prisoner of the media and willful ignorance. He is an Everyman, who lives in a culture that started out with Christianity and now resides in Trump. And he is a survivor:

> survivors: burn the heart
> then pull the soul
> up from the coals
> lighting the straw
> and vestments

he admonishes in *Her Second Lives, and Such*, while adding in *The Star Puppets*

> We watched in dumbstruck lassitude,
> like couch potato marionettes.

In our sleeping state, the state in which we spend most of our lives, he repeatedly tells us we take the word for others as to what has happened around us rather than actually watching, listening to each other, reading, and working to save ourselves. I am going to close this introduction by leaving you with three brilliant but horrifying segments from the closing poem in Life's Prisoners. Note how the first two segments argue over what happened vs. what was reported, and how the final segment drives us home:

               legend has it the man
was lynched, noosed, his flesh charred
unrecognizably as afterbirth,
his clothes tossed to the rags
of history, an oil-soaked human torch…

…The family approaches. To read a plaque,
I guess. Naw. The garden fence is only
to protect the tree, maybe,
from pests, locusts, and *blank* odd threats.

…Now the story is a retired flag
folded up, till it flaps in the breeze
occasionally it snaps like a pocketbook
the tongue clucks like a pocketbook.
My life beneath the limb of a story
playing a stranger's
part in a dumbstruck village
is over. The present begs a way to live
                    together here.

This is what it is to be a man or a woman: to no longer be dumbstruck and silent and sleeping, but to live among those we are fortunate enough to live among.

Life's Prisoners

Life's Prisoners

If I can breakfast with them
then I can frugal repast with you.
If I can socialize at the early table with them
and trade throat lozenges in between the laughter
then I can share planetary accoutrements
and iron chains
with you…
Sad that you make it so difficult.
Whoever you are,
and this will make the second time I have caught you,
speak, speak, speak to me in sighs instead of
perusing my mail.

The World's First Black Gay Sci-fi Writer Devours the Classroom

To Samuel Delany

He needed a black/ gay muse. From
Mars. Launch pad. Blast off. Moon Shits
— that's *shots*, marking it, such bad taste
He coveted like porn exhumed on Saturn.
For red light zone phrases he'd misread
Any error. His bias: Texts are viral —
Chewing on a yummy while he insists
Systems always matter.
            Note: on fictive worlds
— if plotted with a sense of style —
Systems vary: air, earth, water, blue skies
And sand crystals. Stare out a window —
The real world's as pied as prose,
In silence and storm, how language seesaws
In a wild weft of schema heterodox.

The Crippled, Homeless Woman Speaks

Her plea at last uncontained.
God, why are you doing this?
Released past the fury and rain.
The major key is faith.
I can't believe He said that?
The minor chord is disbelief.
She confronts me.
Before I can respond, she groans,
Didn't you hear what He said?
Did He really say something?
Did I miss Him then?
You're crazy. I didn't hear anything.

The Third Trimester

Past-due in the forthcoming hour –
Galvanized. Begun without fair consideration
for bric-a-brac and mortar –
like a combustible high school project.

The Daily Globe

The words rise. Like angels in heaven, sent
to make communion with the neighbors.
In twos. In cherubic threes. In choral fourths.
Sweetheart. *Have you been well?*
I push aside our summer sheets, hoping
to flash sufficient light and dark to catch the intentions
at dawn. Our house no less a parlor than a church
of living bones. The sunlight is pitched funeral dust
spreading peace on earth. I am called by others
living namelessly nearby. To spend my short eternity
imagining addresses. The globe. Every morn it spins
showing any blinkered eye its favorite colors
like a summoning forth.
Today the countries may reveal faces: their hells
blurring with paradises, land, ocean,
Sweden's wealth and China's poor genuflected. The situation
of a world in crisis while limbs lurch
playing at bed sheets and snores and mirrors; let's touch –
kicking at our sore spots. The words rise; lovers
remake the news. *Are you lovely enough to wake?* Sleeping beauty.

Praise to the Window Blinds

The Lady of the afternoon shades remains
caustically unembarrassed and better on intemperate days,
blinded in summer in winter in spring
she listens to her heart shivering
pop goes the eschatological cherry
bath bubbles rising in the froth
the sun is a succulent *Dairy Queen* malt
The Lady of the afternoon shade preserves
her heart inside a locket and a chain
a big sun today its cream rises to the top
a set of keys a house light an Easter Cross
she cannot slit the blinds   *won't* in the meantime
the last sliver the big sun looking ahead
bad weather   an *Atomic Café* malt tomorrow
The Beatles sang "It's Getting Better All the Time"
She was less unrepentant then
her generation's anthem   flotsam and jetsam
the brightness is a peeping Tom shady lady
before her midday stab at reading *The Lord of the Rings*
Easter Sunday coming   a futureless orange peel morn.

Strippers Redux

Evening descends like long black hair
unbundled. And beneath the Empyrean stairs
three gold teeth,
lipstick, a thin, cherry red smile,

and impervious iron hips, Jesus,
drum   drum   tirelessly thumping
the front stage

Jesus may not have liked it much less loved it –

gals strutting airs as lusterless as martyrdom

Junk heap Magi. Goddess of redneck dives.
Goddess of Georgia hinterlands. Lord,
Death won't catch me
before the come-hither gals
blazoning disco lights instead of clothes

such devil-may-care.

***

and every night at *Club Tahiti*
a block away from *Downtown Lounge*
a first burlesque startles like a vampire bat
smoldering at the window, a silhouette in wingspan
plastered over the exit sign.

No escape. No ascensions.

***
    – la, la, la, again tonight,
Lawd-have-mercy steeped inside her emaciated bones
a breastless wonder will join me after dark
fishing from her straps and spangled hose
private pockets
covert interiors on a lark
a photo or two of the family and kids
the crappy kinfolks,
that old man with water on the brain
whose treatments she funds on the installment
           plans
per 1st of the month   per dry fuck   per lap dance
pouts in silence hoping for me to proffer
nickel words
no words
moist words
lucky words
the benedictions that haven't brought me
any better answers

New Letters. Old Advice.

To Roy LaGrone's young daughter

   This is a lonely bachelor's advice.
      Of course.
Consider the world's letters in unsinged bales.
     Prepare her novice heart to taste the mails.
Tell her to memorize the letters
     before setting the bonfires. Burn the majority
like dead spring leaves. Then watch the breeze –
     The smoke. The plumes. Air the study rooms
between writing rebuttals. Take second breaths
     between lick and stamp. Sigh. Value
missives, kindness and kindling. Post
     hoping to receive fewer back. I myself receive
too many offering the best advice
     I already know to give myself:
Dear Little Miss LaGrone. Against probability –
Do not cast the pearls before swine
And always believe against possibility
in time.

Concerning the Recent Brutality

10 pm. Stopped. Frisked.

One Man cries *I Am I Am*
in ecstasy and terror   *I Am*
as the Lord cried
to Moses. Three men
decline to listen
ignoring a sensibility
behind prophesy. A nearby
parking meter winks
metallically on a lightless
street corner. Witnessing
nothing. Glittering
after dark. Stands
like a watch
-tower going senile
totteringly decadent
on duty to collect
poised to pinch
the nickels and dimes
the irrevocable fines
the regular tariffs
blind to the charges of citizenship.

***

ii. The Falling Man
          for Eric Garner
I can't breathe.
I can't see.
My body like a broken
cigarette

crushed fallow
busted loose
cops pick at me
for a chew

Cops finger me like an idle
Parliament. An off-duty
throwaway smoke
spent then discarded.

Tobacco still smooth –
soothing, breathable,
all smokes considered.
A life still *Camel Unfiltered*

still usable. Boots
steel-toed and prescriptive
snipe at the edges
of a *Marlboro Man* –

Light me up.
Throw me down
like a flat-tired
Lucky Strike. Like a sparkle

soon forgotten.
Long time now.
Long time gone. No
news on the horizon –

since 'fore I was born,
'fore I struck light
men have been falling
the preachers the politicians

falling man falling
like past-due checks
the preachers the prideful
the banksters the big

pockets the bigger they are
the harder they. Noses
bloodied bones brittle
crackling clattering

like castanets.
Pull me loose
like the least of the
cards in the house –

falling any red card flashes
in royal pinstripes or
scarlet pantaloons, baby,
baby, least don't say

however frankly I've come a long way.
Pall Malls consumed. Tossed.
I can't breathe. I maybe still burn.
A short life a passable smoke
embering. Less than a matchstick
less, less than a *Lucky Strike*.

The Silence Before the Summer Storm

Before the lightning flashes
a sudden heavy silence scoured poutily bruised
loose lips. We postponed by promising
ourselves clean thoughts and flossing stained
teeth. Bright as spring leaves. Depression apples!
Did I mention the separate sinks: oh, and mirrors!
Still. I managed the scant few July and August
conversations with her nippily arguing
the ineffably petty details out
of the blue, or the dark, and quickly then
the impromptu, childish lies. Quickly then –
The silences before the summer bolts
locking shut the major/minor doors.
The healthy air stymied between the cracks.
The refrigerator hums. A remarkable dirge.
The vapidly green grapes lie in the fridge
like soggy, rotten proof.
And proof. And proof.
Our words, like our repasts together,
going putrid.

Parables for the End of the First Chapter.

Let him fly, let him fly, let him fly, like God's voice. Let a squirrel fly up alongside a crazy bird. The crying bird's lost in the high branches. The foolish man says on a day as azure as today they should have chosen high heaven.

There is a foolish man pursuing God's voice – where else, where else – up a tree – like a root and an intellectual axis.

God must be a bird, beast, or talon. A man's a restless, broke-winged spirit. Lord, Lord, he is too human. *If an eye offend thee pluck it out. Kree kree,* he cries, offended by his whole body. Fleshly. And featherless.

Spits into his palm. Hasn't he bruised five nimble fingers? He scrambles, clambers a branch gnawed by corrosive ants. His animal spirit nature strengthening foothold, by foothold. A squirrel rustles the greenery. Shoots like a motion of light, loss, a revelation's flash. A branch frays. A nervous, blurry *kree kree kree* disrupts the sky.

And he realizes he may have chased his companions away. The bird flown to summer climes. The flocks migratory. Black V's lining greyish horizons, incognito. The squirrel having quit the high home, leaf, bramble, bark, vine, and busily, instinctively digging up the sod below, just another seasonal hibernation.

Snow Blankets the Eastern Hills

Come look. From the balcony.
If you shudder and cough
a moment later you'll sigh.
Tell me. Is sister sleeping?
Is the landscape weeping?
Is Abigail peeking? This landscape
so bleak and stiflingly echolalic –
Is a white carpet worth a wintry
hemisphere? –
     frost's babbling brook
but mutely monochromatic apocalyptic.
Nearer. Come see the view
nearer the pith.
This may be
     maybe   *may be*
what sleep
is like.

Time Travel Haiku

To slip days away.
To brew a gentle coffee –
Add a dumb pink pill.

How weirdly hours fray,
like drifts of furry cotton
- seed in golden haze.

Centuries dissolve.
Clock-time is an aspirin,
crumbling illusions.

Ancient slavery;
Backs broken to build castles,
Bondage to time's lash.

Returned to *polis*.
Stands before fate's Sphinx, sex, death,
Morality's pulse.

Calvary's crude Cross.
To search lost time to affirm
Hour and act. No luck.

He visited tombs
– of grand futures, or grey past?
Vaults of near stasis.

Tick, Tock, Tock, his arc
The farther beyond the pale
Confounds stone and ice.

This way mists to that:
The future's grand glistening
Towers of star daze

Resemble rank caves;
Translucent cities of glass
Seem primal, hot ash.

Sibyl tea leaf flakes
Ashen to kindling; soundless
Apoca-eclipse.

Compressing breakers,
Beyond flash lunar epochs,
Time harvests dusk, dust.

Her Second Lives, and Such

Phoenixes have the loveliest irises
   pupils fired inside cauldrons: the blank
      intensity: the fractured layers undevastated:
         eyes of hurricane glass: shaken storm

survivors: burn the heart
  then pull the soul
    up from the coals
      lighting the straw
and vestments.

Pair funeral pyres and indestructible gems.
  Pair second lives and set jewels.
Phoenixes still have fixed and lovely and
  shrewd and penetrating gazes.
     Reborn watchful and blinded.

Naming the Seasons

the puzzle : the answer to the riddle is man,
    because man is the name behind the naming...

Name a bird that spots its light and late reflections
makes manifold calculations
is thoughtlessly inspired
cannot see its future trees
appreciates inclement weather
and lingers on the present
like a perverse vanity mirror...
simultaneously its own self and clueless.
    Name it.
        Then describe its mating call
a little past noon. Too many species and stripes.
Too many classifications and kinds.
Too many suspect birds.
Another slips beneath a shadow
of spring and summer
glides the translucent and occasional
the thick and less thick
unraveling and aboriginal
dappled-dark seeking
its thoughtlessness like food.

An Aubade

You do not know your hands,
if at all. Not the way you personally believe—
hands, picking lint off imaginary
suits, while wringing psychological towels.
Hands. Leaving marks like a web-making
spider, a body turban, a tight flesh mask
over hollow, bloodless husks of courtesy.
You have been paused too long now
between an urge to touch with grace, without feeling.
You tend to trust too much, although
the slightest simple wave hello, goodbye,
is leveled as a magician's trick,
flashing like cold thin coins worn
faceless, shown, spun, balanced,
flipped, *hello, goodbye*, surreptitiously, then lost up clever sleeves.

The Star Puppets

The nightmare was neither bad television,
nor *kitsch*. Whatever it was struck home
light years away. Something blurrily animal, lissomely human,
blurrily moving, a semblance, a leprechaun,
spidered a hush hush mystery screen
too swiftly to pinpoint the family of man's shadow.
The imagery was archetypal before it was born
on an ancient tree, and the cradle broken
shattering the old limb. A Tree of Knowledge –
Yggdrasil, man's tree of family and faith, ablaze,
ashing, ashing the route to satellite wonders.
Or were we broadcasting ourselves?

We watched in dumbstruck lassitude,
like couch potato marionettes
shoulder to shoulder, locked knees,
mouths puckering up-down, open and shut.
Which way was the root? Whither the star trail?
– switch stations, and Sybil's leaves respelled the fable.
We returned to catch the last theatrical
curtains flying up. Forgive us please stunned expressions –
forgive us silent prayers, rickety
stiffness of trolls on an old geezer's shelf
who thought we trembled given a pair of loose nails
straining the racks.

We burnt like wood. Firewood.
Pinewood. Redwood. Cedar conflagrations
seared ourselves to our skins. Matchstick trees
hung on lean strings of bark and vein
together. A shock so ironic, so homely, so
astral. Picking up a cup, the cabinet cups,

we said *thank you, please*, and lay the saucer down
with the caution of house domestics; forgive us the
      star puppetry –

Color of scalding. Pink flesh of kindling.

          love less love than a skittish
          theatre of strained affections.

Toothpicks. Timber. Cuttings. Shaved saplings.
Teeth to a forestry Nova.

Come Join the Dark

Come join the family darks
who graduated the public schools, skulls dilated
as large as exotic house plants. So
far everything in life has grown from
seed, watering. There has been bitterness, too,
in the night, nights of too many
stark tears, the darkness a peculiar
skittering, skittering in the ceiling—
shy as a vanishing fawn; dark the fabled tree
where a stillborn baby was buried
dark in a shoe box somewhere back
that you have heard rumored since
a marvelous family get together when Uncle Lee
drank so much he took a pee
      and out of his piss sprang the first flowers of spring.

But if someone who was nobody's brother or
sister's favorite foolish foil sisterly meddled
in the middle of a fabulous story, inces-
tuous inbreeding, stolen kisses beneath
flowering trees, animal gropings in the hay,
shit, mush, pig crust underneath the straw,
a mouth twisted in disgust like a backwards cap,
he would be handed a gravedigger's shovel
unwashed from a throwaway pile and pointed
in a dark direction; he would be told
—*sorry*, they whispered and gestured, *see*—
to do the job that was too dark for you or me.

Dubois at 90

for Jim Campbell's 90th anniversary

When W.E.B. looked back on salad days –
so-called: revolving: evolving: history in the making
the vagaries of events spread like dominos
in play. History's black and white dice rolled. Oceanic
possibilities bobbed like shipwrecked hulls.
He looked back on Titanic tribulations weathered
pell-mell. From tailor shops to modern tanks.
The *fin de siècle's* severed horse and carriage –
The post-war movements as they crested on the waves
and liberated a few from the unintelligible
politics of rage. He studied each new print edition
like braille. By his fingers' touch he read
A 19th century's lost pastoral; the 20th's impenetrable
                              armor –
From divergent paths he gleaned a centre axis.
The way you wake to today and tomorrow's headlines.
Today and tomorrow's interpretations.

***

Dear Jim. Explicator of history's long haul –
Penetrator of DNA science and revolutionary hearts –
Taking a leaf from hawk, musical oriole, the haunted dove,
Tell me again the fault that lingers is in ourselves
 – like a stifled lyre in accord with private error.
Tell me with your voice like a melodious viol
the newspaper dawn swivels on a sharper axis
of hope. The propagandistic 21st century terrors
still obey a trajectory. Take away *The New York Times'*
poisonous cup. Too murky to be trusted –
Coming into your 90th year's still disciplined glory –
Tell me the truth is as transparent as water, as water,
as air, *as air*. And instill in me the news of the future.
Fill me. Fill me in, Jim. Man's inside story.

To Ellison/Baldwin

***

First words. Written. As quickly they
Vanish. Like ink in slow burn to air.
How really can a man leave proof?
For one novel earth and air settled
Into a shape like a lonely cloud
In metals. An iron cast so solid
A soul could breathe inside its chest.
That soul stays unnamed. He is All
Or all who pause to wisely hear
His voice. His story is of choices
– some he can see, others darkly assumed.
The options swish him in a ronde,
Wise man, Slave, Fool? No straw man.
Touch him, the flesh warms. An invisible.

***

You'll always return. You tried risking love
Beyond the room. Its walls called like
Angels will: when they appear in dreams
– all bottled up inside a fantasy so
Private the wings knock like paper planes,
Crying while singing such mangled, airless arias.
Neither the songs they've horded nor cherish.
No better angels would be caught dead
— ah what men propose, irony will dispose—
In Giovanni's room. The kinds of prayers
They know of still are settled here
– yes, but the touch is rough, rash,
Leaving an imprint like a whore's ruse:
Love. I am happy to see you.

The First Photographs

  – bellies pallid   swimmingly transparent
fishy-mouthed
less phlegmatic than filmy
a wormy, intractable iridescence
as piquant as caviar eggs   an everlasting gloaming
at shore side   shiny all over
soulless all under
crawling like slugs
near the rocks sullen.
Running in schools
flecked silvery –
harvested beneath bone white
sheds, semi-precious, elemental,
more perfect than stone
washed of celestial excess
richly polished
a space age aquatic –
Our palms blanched
colorless as asteroids
craggily knuckled and witless.
We put them down: our Bibles,
the bulk bulging, spreading
lachrymosely wet sheets, wet, slick papyri,
then lifted our hands.

And They Say

I heard there was a legend
nearby. I only see a Spanish oak.
Neither death nor the sun...
Nature's Golgotha. Or a green Ragnarok.
A church letting out. A family
vanishing into the block.
I kind of detest the blaze of legend
less pure than simple lies.
It may be gossip's swiftest
avenue to retooling its alibi
for cruelty...

        legend has it the man
was lynched, noosed, his flesh charred
unrecognizably as afterbirth,
his clothes tossed to the rags
of history, an oil-soaked, human torch.
His body was a clock
broken by drunken sailors,
slammed against a brick wall, loosening
the memory of pain's instruments.
The charts.

He was twisted beneath a limb
preserved in a square on blank street,
the oak still living, serpentine, Gothic,
longer than any accusatory finger.
The family approaches. To read a plaque,
I guess. Naw. The garden fence is only
to protect the tree, maybe,
from pests, locusts, and *blank* odd threats.

The victim was blinded first.
He was a soldier… his heirs, his relatives…
say this, say that…. Or who says much
beside the steady erosion of *tic, tock*.
Trace his body in civic sands.
Trace a memorial in the public dust.
This is a Maypole Sunday. Adults
matter less than esplanade children,
kids still matter more than strangers.

Not oak nor ivy could make the tale
charming. Or make a case history *isn't*
playground rumor. I shouldn't say that
anyhow. No matter the last, surviving witness
stands like a testimony which faintly
incriminates: like silences after a death.
I guess the dead inhale. Exhale. Like memory's breath.
Pretend the oak tree called for a funeral hush.
Pretend happenstance may someday honor it
like a storm which turns away from a ghost house,

a lull flickering. *And they say…*
An outline: rumor, legend, gossip is a contour
A profile in sidewalk chalk, a bag of bones.
None of the skeletal anatomy filled in
nor veins. Children may crayon it in colorfully.
I heard about a fable woman, conjuress,
slave, though she was real, neither, both,
 – I still know she was black, no rites
of the festooned macabre changed *that*.
Probably talked too much. They said.

A human scarification. Her lips sewn shut.
Guess she was *alive*, her nasty fibs
punished. Now the story is a retired flag
folded up, till it flaps in the breeze
occasionally it snaps like a pocketbook
the tongue clucks like a pocketbook.
My life beneath the limb of a story
playing a stranger's
part in a dumbstruck village
is over. The present begs a way to live
       together here.

Acknowledgments

"The Daily Globe," "The Star Puppets," "Strippers Redux," "Life's Prisoners," and "10pm. Stopped. Frisked." originally appeared in *Mad Swirl*

"An Aubade," "The Falling Man," and "The Silence before the Summer Storm," originally appeared in *Turtle Island Quarterly*

"Time Travel Haiku" originally appeared in *Pedestal Magazine*

"The First Photographs" originally appeared in *Zephyr*

"To Ellison/Baldwin" originally appeared in *Rigorous*

"New Letters. Old Advice" and "Dubois at 90" originally appeared in *The Voices Project*

"The World's First Black Gay Sci-fi Writer Devours the Classroom" originally appeared in *Radius*

"Come Join the Dark" originally appeared in *Boston Review*

"And They Say" originally appeared in *Matter Monthly*

Photo of the author reading the poem "And They Say"

Darryl Lorenzo Wellington has spent 20 years as a journalist, syndicated columnist, playwright, poet, surrealist, and performance artist. His essays on poverty, economic justice, race relations, African American history, civil rights history, and post-Katrina New Orleans have appeared in *The Nation, The Progressive, The Christian Science Monitor, The Atlantic, Dissent, The Washington Post, Equal Voices, Common Dreams, Crisis (The NAACP magazine), Huffington Post, N+1, Talk Poverty, The Guardian*, and the *Billmoyers.com* website. He has appeared as a guest on the *Tavis Smiley Radio Show*. He has published poetry in *Turtle Island Quarterly, Pedestal, Matter Monthly, Drunken Boat, Boston Review,* and other places. He is presently a Writing Fellow at the Center for Community Change in Washington, DC, and in the arts (sometimes in life) he loves playing with fire.

www.ingramcontent.com/pod-product-compliance
Lightning Source LLC
Chambersburg PA
CBHW050336120526
44592CB00014B/2205